Manage Your Anxiety and Stress

MANAGE YOUR ANXIETY AND STRESS

Mariad Burke
& Dr Phil Robert

Burke Robert Publishing Ltd

Manage Your Anxiety and Stress

Second edition © 2013
Text © 2013 by Mariad Burke & Dr Phil Robert
Illustrations © 2012 by Teresa Howes
Edited by Rena McDonald & Dr Carmel Larkin
Published by Burke Robert Publishing Ltd., Dublin, Ireland

All rights reserved.
No part of this book may be used or reproduced in any manner without written permission of the publisher, except in the case of brief quotations embodied in critical articles and reviews.

Cover design by Karina Robert & Owen Brady

ISBN: 978-1-909393-10-3

Printed at Picatype Systems Pvt Ltd, Pune

www.burkerobertpublishing.com

To

Kathleen, Jimmy & Jackie

Manage Your Anxiety and Stress

Foreword

This ***Empower Yourself Series*** of books evolved as a common sense step by step approach to personal dilemmas that can happen to anyone, at any time, during their lifetime. Our aim is to reach as many people as possible in order to help them to empower themselves.

You are the person best qualified to identify what you need to live a happy and satisfying life. In these books we aim to provide you with essential information and therapy skills to enable you to deal with your immediate problem on a 24/7 basis.

Think of these books as a toolbox that will assist you in building up your own skills and in so doing, help you to use the talents you have to deal with what is presently causing anxiety and stress in your life.

Each book in the series is a stand-alone, single problem solution based therapy aid.

The strategies outlined in this series can be used by anyone as needed throughout their life, regardless of gender, culture, religion, political affiliations, ethnicity or sexual orientation.

However, we stress that this book is not an alternative to prescribed medication, nor is it designed to replace medical interventions, but rather to support them.

Those considering therapy, or those who have no knowledge or experience of therapy whatsoever, or who are fearful of what therapy involves, will benefit greatly from the books in the ***Empower Yourself Series***.

Each book in the ***Empower Yourself Series*** is also a helpful reference / guide to those who are already in therapy.

The strategies and information outlined in these books will give the reader an insight into what happens during counselling sessions. This in turn will reduce the mystery, stigma and fear-factor often associated with the counselling process.

Mental health and physical health are both essential for well-being. Physical health is associated with physical fitness and well-being. There is no stigma attached to attending a medical practitioner when physically ill with the expectation of a positive outcome.

When it comes to mental health the same rule should apply. However, mental health issues are often seen in a less positive light.

If mental health issues are given the same attention as physical ailments, they also can have a positive outcome.

Embracing the strategies detailed in the ***Empower Yourself Series*** will empower you on a personal level and will also promote both your physical / mental health and well-being and improve every part of your life.

Manage Your Anxiety and Stress

Manage Your Anxiety and Stress

Contents

Introduction 1

Part 1
Anxiety / Stress 7
What is stress? 8
Categories of stress 10
What are your stressors? 13
First step in easing stressful anxiety 15
Breathing exercises 16
Reframe the situation using humour 17
Talk about your situation 18
Journaling 20
Time management 25
Worry period 27
Sleep 28
Develop the skill of relaxation 34

Part 2
Exercise 43
Mindfulness 50
Meditation 57

Religion and Spirituality 60
It's your choice 63

Part 3
Basic human needs common to all 67
Healthy lifestyle choices 68
Evaluate your belief system 70
Changing your thinking 74
Overcome the power of negative thinking ... 80
Effective communication 85
Challenge yourself 88
Continuous evaluation 92
Summary 94
Illustrator 97
Empower Yourself Series 98

Manage Your Anxiety and Stress

Introduction

This series evolved because of the needs expressed by clients during counselling sessions. Many clients benefit from a step by step approach to resolving their own issues. This series encapsulates this step by step approach in hard copy to enable individuals to pick up at a time of their own choosing.

Another reason for this series is that many people lead busy lives and cannot commit to attend weekly counselling sessions. This has led them to experience feelings of isolation and helplessness.

From our own experience, and that of other professionals in the field, we observed the prevailing issues that arise in counselling. The main issues generally centre round relationship difficulties, which are often caused by underlying personal problems.

We designed this series to address specific personal dilemmas in such a manner as to give reassurance, hope and empowerment to individuals, who understand that they are best placed to change their own behaviour.

This *Empower Yourself Series* could be compared to a first aid kit, which not only empowers the individual who experiences the specific issue, but also helps those around them to understand their issues and help them in their quest to heal themselves.

Education is empowering in itself. It also helps those who have partners or family members or close associates, who are struggling with mental health issues, to understand the underlying problem.

When close associates familiarise themselves with the *Empower Yourself Series*, they will be motivated to generate discussion with the person who is encountering the mental health issue. This collaboration promotes the necessary changes required for positive outcomes.

Our aim in writing these books is to strip out all non-essentials and provide the individual with what they need, in a simple, easy to understand, jargon-free fashion, when it is required. These books are intentionally brief and concise.

In case of relapse or stressful times, these books can be picked up again and the step by step process repeated.

The books are written as if we as counsellors are engaging on a one to one basis with you the reader, addressing the specific issue named in the title.

We hope that putting the contents of these books into action will empower you and help you to fulfil your needs.

Manage Your Anxiety and Stress

Part 1

Manage Your Anxiety and Stress

Anxiety / Stress

This book integrates many therapies, but it does not seek to explain them.

Since creation, all creatures of the universe, including humans, have an inbuilt instinct for fight / flight or freeze in order to survive.

If your stress / anxiety is causing you problems and you are not managing it effectively, then this book is for you. It provides you with the tools required to help you get through each day.

It is a solution based, common-sense approach, easy to use, by anyone experiencing problems managing their stress / anxiety.

The aim of this book is to provide you with the coping strategies necessary to manage your anxiety and stress and to deal with normal stress, which is a part of everyday living.

This process will take time and effort. By practising the methods outlined in this book, you will no longer allow anxiety and stress to hold you back. Your life will become more manageable, enjoyable and much less frightening.

What is stress?

Stress is a natural reaction, which helps us cope when certain events place strong demands on us, in the course of our everyday lives. Accidents, financial problems, work related problems and family related issues all lead to stress.

With proper coping skills, the average person meets their stressful challenges head-on and aspires to achieve their full potential. Some people thrive on stress and it motivates them to get things done.

Stress / anxiety can affect your interaction with friends and family, your working relationships and adversely disrupt the overall quality of your life.

Studies have also revealed that stress triggers panic attacks, irritable bowel syndrome, somatic illnesses, phobias, post-traumatic stress disorder, addictions, suicidal ideation, self-harm, low self-esteem, cancer and many other debilitating conditions.

Stress can manifest itself in sweating, palpitations, rapid heart-beat, faintness, dizziness, dry mouth, shaking, crying, shouting etc.

Your body produces cortisol and adrenalin in order to energise itself to face stressful events. Your body needs to relax between stressful episodes, otherwise your over-stressed body is continuously producing cortisol and adrenalin.

Unless you learn to manage your stress effectively you will burn-out and this in turn will affect your mental and physical health.

Stress affects everyone differently and therefore requires a wide range of different coping strategies. You will choose the strategies which work best for you in your given situation.

It is impossible to eliminate stress from your life, but it is imperative that you learn the skills necessary to deal with it.

By effectively managing your stress on an on-going basis, you improve and expand your coping skills and your life / health improves accordingly.

Categories of stress

The following is a list of categories of stressors. These are not exclusive and are often interlinked. Stress / anxiety in one area can effect or damage other areas of your life.

Family / relationships

Some of the stressful factors involved in family and close personal relationships include, extra-marital affairs, parenting, caring for elderly relatives, rebellious teenagers, unwanted pregnancies, pets, bereavements, finance, ill health, substance abuse, addictions and / or violence.

Stress in this core area of your life creates a major impact on family relationships and as a consequence you carry it with you into other areas of your life.

Work related stress

The workplace is a stressful environment involving interpersonal relationships, deadlines, pressures of learning new skills and technologies, job security, performance and financial considerations.

Environmental

The stressors in this area are wide-ranging and can include noise disturbance, pollution, moving house, emigrating, weather disturbances, technology, new job, local community, neighbours, global warming, animal welfare, nuclear threats, religious and political issues, war, oppression, powerlessness, world health and economic issues, etc.

Financial stress

Financial difficulties are a major source of stress. This stress affects every other area of your life. It prevents you fulfilling many of your obligations and in turn affects your family and your physical and mental health.

Health

Health problems are a major source of stress. Stress in this area ranges from sleeplessness, to addictions, to terminal illnesses. When a family member is ill, it impacts on all other family members, whether the illness is short-term, long-term or terminal.

The stress experienced by caregivers has enormous effects on their physical and mental well-being. Caregivers must learn to take care of themselves first and incorporate regular periods of respite into their lives.

Stress can lead to illness and illnesses can cause stress.

Psychological stress

Differences in cultural backgrounds, ethnicity, religious and political beliefs and / or certain social activities can be major causes of stress. Irrational fears and phobias are examples of psychological stress. Psychological stress can lead to somatic illnesses.

What are your stressors?

Stress is part of everyday life. Two people observing the same event will experience different thoughts about it. Your own personal perception defines your reality, triggers your feelings and as a consequence your responses.

Visualise two football supporters at a football match, each supporting opposing teams. One team scores, one supporter is elated while the other is deflated.

This is just a simple example of different responses to the same event. It also illustrates how hobbies and interests can alleviate stress while at the same time add to it.

What triggers stress in your daily life? It could be a minor issue such as someone not replacing the cap on the toothpaste, or a major issue like facing bankruptcy.

Stress is a build-up of intense feelings usually related to a combination of things.

Use a notepad to jot down your stressors. Evaluate your response to the stressor.

Is your response disproportionate to the event? If so, can you do something about it?

For example, if you are in financial difficulties, approach your lender and discuss your difficulties. This action will ease your stress and help you to feel more in control of your situation.

Based on your observations of your stressors, ask yourself are you a person whose glass is half full or half empty?

Do you look on the bright side of life or are you inclined to be negative?

Pessimistic people tend to be more stressed.

Worry cannot in itself change any situation, but it can lead to stress.

Worrying is self-defeating and its negative effects are only felt by the worrier.

However, you can teach yourself to develop optimistic thinking, which is the mind's self-defence against worry and stress.

This is easier said than done. So how do you go about retraining your thinking process in order to alleviate your stress?

First step in easing stressful anxiety

Where possible take time-out i.e. find a quiet secure place away from the immediate incident causing your elevated stress.

If possible, request a trusted other person to accompany you.

Take stock of what your body is telling you. Monitor your level of anxiety on a scale of 1 to 10, with 10 being the highest.

Use the following breathing exercises whenever you are feeling stressed or anxious, when your breathing is fast and shallow, your pulse is racing or you feel dizzy or faint.

Ground / compose yourself fully, using the following techniques and notice your level of anxiety reduce, before resuming your usual activities.

Breathing exercises are the key to interrupting your negative or worrying thoughts with immediate effect.

Breathing exercises

Breathing exercises are fast acting techniques to help you feel better quickly.

Laboured breathing or shallow breathing causes stress in itself. It is important to breathe from your diaphragm.

Take deep breaths through your nose, concentrating on the air going into your lungs.

Notice your breath going deep down into your tummy and feel your tummy expanding.

Exhale slowly through your mouth and feel your tummy relaxing as you exhale.

Say the word **RELAX** as you breathe out.

Practise this on a regular basis for even greater benefits.

It may help you to breathe into a bag or your cupped hands.

By concentrating on your breathing, you are no longer focusing on stressful thoughts.

Reframe the situation using humour

Have you ever looked back at a stressful experience and laughed about it when shared with a friend? Humour helps to ease stressful situations for example, when going for an interview you could imagine the interviewers naked!

Do you see the funny side of others' stressful dilemmas when described to you? Try to apply this reframing from a humorous perspective to your own dilemmas.

Think of numerous comedy sketches. Comedians make successful careers by making fun of stressful situations all of the time. So, get into the habit of looking on the funny side whenever possible. Laughter and humour lighten the load.

Appropriate humour can be effective in lightening your mood, diffusing a stressful situation, relaxing the muscles and is basically good for you.

Humour is infectious, brings us close to other people and also satisfies our need for fun.

Talk about your situation

Discussing your stressors with someone you trust, can help you clarify your thoughts and feelings surrounding the stressful event. Their feedback also allows you to see things from a different perspective.

Talking about your feelings eases stress. It is equivalent to releasing pressure from a pressure cooker before it builds up to dangerous levels.

Focus on the following areas:

What is the evidence?

What is the evidence to either support or deny your stressful thoughts?

Do you listen to alternative views?

How do others view this situation and how would you advise someone in the same situation as yourself?

Is your thinking flawed?

Are you always focusing on the negative, blaming yourself or jumping to conclusions?

What action can you take to alleviate the situation?

Women have a great capacity for discussing their problems openly. This is as beneficial for their mental health as exercise is for their physical health.

On the other hand, some men tend to form relationships around activities rather than their personal lives. They could benefit greatly through connecting with others differently.

Forming and maintaining close interpersonal relationships is a necessary component for both males and females and provides a support system for easing and managing stress.

Journaling

Journaling is writing down your thoughts and feelings and is healing in itself. It is a good idea to get into the habit of writing a personal journal. Make sure to find a safe place where you feel comfortable and secure to express your innermost thoughts and let off steam about the situations and people impacting on you in your life.

Your journal is private to you and in order to be of benefit, you must feel positive that it is not open to prying eyes. Sharing your journal entries with others is not necessarily a good idea, as it puts undue pressure on you to be conscious of the reader's reactions.

Journaling can only be therapeutic if you are free to be totally honest in expressing your emotions, fears, dreams, aspirations and include the good, the bad and the ugly. You don't need to impress anyone else with your journal entries. It is yours and yours alone. You are writing for yourself, so you have no need to be fearful of others judging you.

Date all entries and feel free to express your thoughts on what is happening in your life.

Perhaps you would like to play music in the background. Your choice of music alone is an indicator of how you feel at that particular moment. Perhaps you will choose to write a single word on the page, or draw an image.

If you are not artistic, cut out an image from a magazine to represent your thoughts, feelings or hopes for the future. This picture, of itself, will paint a thousand words.

Use an alarm and give yourself five minutes to write down whatever is in your head. You are entitled to spend five minutes for yourself.

If you notice an unusual length of time between journal entries, this is also indicative of what is happening to you in your life i.e. you are busy, on holiday, too preoccupied to put pen to paper, or any number of reasons. Write in a completely non-judgemental fashion. You are entitled to feel the way you do.

Journaling is an excellent therapeutic exercise when experiencing grief, or going through a divorce or separation, especially if you are trying to keep a brave face in order to support or protect vulnerable people around you.

It may be useful to write 'unsent letters' to people who are no longer with us, or 'dialogues' with those with whom we have unfinished business.

Journaling is very constructive. It is amazing how we often look back at the past with different eyes as a result of events that occurred in the intervening time.

Journaling allows you to return to the felt emotions at the time of the occurrences and helps you to re-evaluate the real situations as they unfolded. Having written a journal entry, take the time to reread it and give yourself some feedback.

Journaling makes you more aware of the strategies you have used and allows you to evaluate your reactions retrospectively.

If you journal your stressful feelings on a regular basis you may become aware of a pattern. Stress causes people to focus on minute trivialities, as opposed to seeing the big picture.

Journaling helps you to alleviate this tendency. Use your journal as your inner coach to employ the lessons you have learned and put them into practise when required.

Make a list of the strategies you have used and congratulate yourself on how far you have come and what you have achieved in managing the stressful occurrences in your life.

Make 'gratitude lists' of all the good things and people in your life for an instant boost.

When you feel stuck, or that your life is like a merry-go-round, your journal helps you to unravel your muddled thinking in a logical, systematic way.

Journaling your stressful thoughts, fears and feelings, is a release valve in itself. It enables you to offload whatever is disturbing you and interfering with your life. Once you acknowledge your thoughts, you are then free to focus on one issue at a time; thus leaving you in a better position to take a step back and take action to deal with each dilemma as required.

Journaling helps you to see yourself as you really are. Your journal is a mirror-image of the real you, warts and all. Many people are so down on themselves that they don't give themselves credit for all that they are.

Your journal will show you just how wonderful you are, how resilient you are and how capable you are at managing the challenges that present themselves in your daily life. It empowers you to learn to love yourself and to act according to your own principles.

In short, journaling will set you free to follow your dreams, unhindered by anyone else's opinions except your own.

Time management

There are major differences in the manner in which people respond to stress. You can choose how stress will affect you in your daily life.

When you worry about getting everything done you tend to focus on your stressors exclusively to the detriment of other areas of your daily life.

Time management and balance are vital components in easing your stress levels.

It is imperative that you set aside sufficient time for work, play, relationships, self-care, exercise and sleep and stick to your plan.

It is beneficial for you to set aside a specific time, a 'worry period' for worrying each day. Choose the same time and the same place daily.

When you notice yourself worrying during the day or night, note it and postpone your worrying until your allocated time. No need to worry about it now, you can address it during your 'worry period'.

You might like to carry a notepad with you as a reminder to jot down your worries to address them later.

Focus on some other area of interest to you as a distraction e.g. doing a crossword, a jigsaw puzzle, watching sport etc. Do something practical, positive or pleasurable.

This strategy of defer, delay and distract may seem a bit strange, but developing this new skill, with time and patience, will prove very effective in empowering you to ease your anxiety and stress.

The secret of time management is planning and organisation. We all know that if you want something done, you ask a busy person. Are you that busy person who can get overloaded with tasks? Learn to delegate and / or to say NO.

It is also important for you to be realistic about your capabilities. Learning to be less rigid and more flexible with your time and attitudes reduces the threat of burn-out.

Putting these strategies into action will help you feel more in control of your life and ease your stress levels.

Worry period

Go to your allocated space at your allocated time e.g. a comfortable warm place with no distractions preferably after 18:00 hours but no later than 21:00 (at least two to three hours before bedtime).

Take out your notes where you have listed your worries during the day. Look through them. You may find that some of them may no longer concern you.

If you need to worry about some of them, make sure you limit your time to each specified worry.

It is also helpful to write your thoughts on paper rather than keep them in your head. Do whatever you find helpful for you.

Plan your actions to address your worries as necessary.

Sleep

Sleep is a basic human need. It is as necessary for our physical and mental well-being as food and water is for our nourishment and normal functioning.

Sleep is far more important than resting. We spend approximately one third of our lives sleeping.

You may need eight hours sleep per night for you to feel rejuvenated, while others may require a lot less.

If you are having difficulty sleeping, understanding the sleeping process will help you to develop positive strategies to improve your sleeping pattern.

There are four stages involved in the sleeping process. Stages one and two, (when you dream) usually last between five and fifteen minutes.

These are the stages when you are "falling asleep", and are easily disturbed or awakened.

Stages three and four are when you sleep deeply. You do not dream during this period of sleep. Stage four is the most essential for your physical and mental well-being as this is the time when your body repairs and rejuvenates itself.

Your body reverts back through the stages, with brief periods of wakefulness in between, of which you are not aware.

Your body programmes itself to ensure that you spend enough time in deep sleep, regardless of the type of day you have had, or the lack of sleep you have had in recent days. Your period of deep sleep usually lasts approximately two hours per night, during which time, your mind restores itself.

Contrary to popular myth, if you have had very little sleep on previous nights, there is no necessity for you to go to bed early to make up for lost sleep.

Your body programme will shorten stages one and two and lengthen stages three and especially stage four the following night, in order to allow your body to repair and rejuvenate.

Your sleep may be disrupted during times of anxiety and stress, panic, fear, anger, illness and heavy responsibilities, but be assured that your body will compensate for this by ensuring that the greatest percentage of your sleeping hours is spent in deep, restorative sleep.

If you have been having problems sleeping and you have been lying awake tossing and turning over a period of time, you may associate the bedroom with anxiety. Worrying about events of the day or anticipating the next day exacerbates the problem, thus further disrupting your attempts to sleep.

So what can you do to rectify this problem?

Now that you understand the four stages of sleep, you are in a better position to monitor your sleeping requirements. Are you over-estimating, or under-estimating your sleeping requirements?

Have you an established bedroom routine?

If insomnia, or lack of sleep, is causing you concern, then in order to improve your sleep pattern, it is important for you to have a bedroom routine and to use your bedroom for sleep and relaxing activities only. In this way your body will associate the bedroom with sleep.

For this reason it is important for you to avoid watching TV, using a computer or phone, eating or problem solving in the bedroom.

Make sure that your room is cool, airy, clean and that your bed is comfortable. This helps induce sleep.

A simple solution, such as hanging dark curtains in your bedroom, can make a big difference to your sleep pattern.

If you are still awake and are worrying or anxious after fifteen minutes, get out of bed and leave your bedroom.

Keep yourself warm and pursue a pre-planned activity i.e. read, or do a jig-saw puzzle, or a crossword in another room until you feel sleepy.

If you have trouble sleeping, don't make up for it in the morning. Set an alarm and aim to get up earlier.

Reducing the time you spend in bed is more beneficial for you in the long run.

Taking a bath before bedtime is also helpful.

Avoid smoking immediately before bedtime or during the night.

Avoid drinking caffeine drinks, or eating heavy meals four to six hours before bedtime.

Caffeine is a diuretic and your sleep will be disturbed if you have consumed too much liquid prior to retiring for the night.

However, it is important to be aware of the importance of hydration.

While you may fall asleep more quickly having consumed alcohol, it also causes you to wake early, resulting in loss of sleep.

A light, milky snack promotes sleep, while late exercise can delay it.

Do not self-medicate. Your doctor may prescribe sleeping pills in the short-term. If so, make sure to take them at the same time every evening as prescribed.

This will help to regulate your sleeping pattern and ensure that you regulate your body clock, so a feeling of tiredness will kick in around the same time every night, when you no longer require medication.

Try not to nap during the day, as this will make it even more difficult for you to sleep at night.

If you feel you must take a nap, set an alarm and do not nap for longer than thirty minutes in total.

Don't engage in mind-challenging experiences before retiring, such as working late, watching harrowing news / films / documentaries etc.

Listen to music, or read a book or a magazine and this may help you to relax.

It is a good idea to jot down your worries in your notepad to be addressed the following day during your worry period, in order to clear your mind before going to bed.

Relax and unwind before you go to bed.

Develop the Skill of Relaxation

Relaxation is a skill that can be learned.

Do you ever feel stressed out and know that you need to relax but insist that you just don't have the time to do so?

When you feel like this, it is the time when you need to take time out, however briefly and relax.

Tension can cause tiredness and irritability.

Do you sometimes feel all tensed up and suffer headaches, backache and other aches and pains, causing you further anxiety worrying about the cause of your symptoms?

It is impossible to feel tense and relaxed at the same time, so learning the skill of relaxation is of great importance to you when you are stressed or anxious.

If you find it difficult to relax, make a decision to learn a few relaxation exercises and make them part of your daily routine.

Find yourself a quiet, airy space where you can relax in comfort without fear of interruption.

Make sure you are not hungry or full from a large meal.

Be cognisant of your age and your state of fitness and do the relaxation exercises that you know suit you.

Here are a few examples of very brief stress management and relaxations techniques.

Breathe slowly in through your nose for the count of four, hold your breath and then exhale through your mouth to the count of four.

When you feel yourself tensing up, just drop your shoulders and relax your body.

Become aware of the way you are holding your head. Hold your head up as if there is an invisible hook at the top of your head holding your head upright. Allowing your head to droop can cause tension headaches.

Imagine that you are picking fruit in an orchard. Raise both arms in the air. First stretch your right arm up as far as it will go, then, do the same with your left arm.

Roll your shoulders forward in a circular motion as far as they will go. Then reverse your shoulder rolls. When you feel you have done enough, shrug your shoulders a few times.

Stretch and yawn regularly. Get into the habit of sitting back in your chair.

Make a fist with your hands. Notice when you are white-knuckled and unclench your fists. You can do this exercise one hand at a time or both together.

Give yourself a relaxing head massage. Support your elbows on your knees and drop your head into your hands. Make yourself comfortable. Massage your head moving your fingertips in a circular motion over your scalp and feel yourself relaxing.

Stretch out your legs, point your toes towards the floor. Feel the tension in the front of your legs, hold that position for the count of ten. Bring your toes back to their normal position and then point your toes upwards towards you. Feel the tension in the back of your legs, holding for the count of ten. Return your feet to their normal position.

This exercise will, when practised regularly, release the heaviness often felt in your legs during stressful times.

Sip a glass of water slowly. This has a dual effect, it allows you to focus on the act of lifting the glass to your mouth and letting the water soothe your throat, thus slowing down your stressful thoughts.

The exercises above, with the exception of the head massage, can be performed either sitting down or standing up.

If you have more time to relax you could try some of the following:

Soak yourself in a luxurious bath with a fragrance or salts of your choice. Epsom salts and lavender are often recommended for relaxation.

Record your favourite musical programme. Turn off the phone. Light a candle, pour yourself a soft drink, relax and enjoy the music.

If the weather is cold, light the fire and sit back and enjoy a book of your choice.

Invite friends around for a barbecue, or just a chat and a laugh. Laughter relaxes all your muscles.

If you want a good belly laugh, watch a comedy on television or rent a DVD of your choice. There is nothing like a good belly laugh to de-stress you.

Stroking a pet is another method of relaxation. If you do not have a pet you can stroke a cushion, something furry or a silky item or whatever material you like e.g. satin, velvet, wood or steel. This will have the effect of slowing down your breathing and lessening your anxiety / stress levels.

Have you ever heard the expression; 'Fake it 'till you make it'?

In terms of stress management, this simply means tensing all your muscles at once, holding them as tensely as you can for as long as you can and then releasing them all at once.

You will feel an instant sense of relief and relaxation.

If you really want to learn the skill of relaxation, put time aside to follow the progressive muscle relaxation exercise which involves tensing and relaxing all the muscles in your body, one group at a time.

You begin with your hands and arms, followed by your shoulders, forehead, eyes, jaw, neck, tummy, thighs, calves, feet and toes.

This exercise will take around fifteen to twenty minutes. You will be amazed at how relaxed you will feel afterwards.

Make a conscious decision to stop rushing around and trying to do everything at once.

Plan your tasks and take short breaks.

Don't push yourself too hard.

Once you adopt a calm relaxed attitude, you will find that you make fewer mistakes and not only get more things done, but you actually enjoy doing them.

Start to think about and spend time with others.

Make time for yourself and build fun into your day.

Manage Your Anxiety and Stress

Part 2

Manage Your Anxiety and Stress

Exercise

There is an old Irish proverb, which states that you'll never plough a field by turning it over in your mind.

The same is true of exercise.

Exercise is an essential part of well-being regardless of age, gender, ability, or disability.

The most essential requirement for a successful exercise regime is motivation.

Once you are motivated and have consulted your medical practitioner with regard to your suitability, you are ready to go.

The longest journey begins with one step.

Your exercise plan must be appropriate to your age, fitness level and ability.

There are suitable exercises for everyone.

Some exercises are included in the *Healthy Lifestyle Choices* and *Develop the Skill of Relaxation* sections of this book and do not need to be repeated here.

Walking is an excellent form of exercise.

You can walk alone, with friends, pets, children or on treadmills, at home walking on the spot, or just generally incorporate walking into your daily routine to get you from place to place.

Try to get into the habit of leaving your car at home and walking short journeys.

When using public transport, get off at the stop before your desired destination, thus building exercise into your day without too much effort on your part.

Begin slowly.

You are not expected to run a marathon or climb Mount Everest.

Begin by walking for ten minutes a day and build on your progress gradually.

In time you could join a walking club.

This will tick a couple of boxes in terms of your overall well-being, such as socialising and adding to your circle of friends, being adventurous, going to new places and making positive changes in your life.

Exercise helps you feel fitter and healthier.

There are numerous forms of exercise and it is up to you to find one that suits your taste and personality.

If you enjoy a solitary lifestyle, then choose an exercise like swimming, archery, cycling, jogging, etc.

If you are a team person, then take up a sports activity such as football, tennis, golf, sailing, etc.

If you are a fun person, dancing could be the exercise for you.

If you have a disability, don't let your disability prevent you from exercising and being fit.

Even if you are confined to a wheelchair, you can increase your blood circulation, lung capacity, strengthen your muscles and ease the discomfort and stiffness you experience, by doing chair exercises.

The following exercises are equally suitable for the older generation.

Get a full tin of food or a small bottle of water.

Take the tin / bottle in one hand or use two tins or two bottles and hold one in each hand if you feel able.

Use these items as weights to build up the strength of your muscles.

Lift them up towards your shoulders as often as it is comfortable for you.

Then relax.

Another simple exercise is to rotate your wrists 360 degrees in both directions to strengthen your hands.

Do the same with your feet, if you are able to.

Tilt your head on to your right shoulder.

Then tilt it on to your left shoulder.

Touch your chest with your head and then raise your head as far backwards as you can.

Finally, rotate your neck in a circular motion; then do the same in the opposite direction.

Sit comfortably and keep your head straight and in the same position for all of the following eye exercises.

Moving your eyes only, look up towards the left as far as you can.

Then look downwards to the right as far as you can see.

Bring your eyes back to the centre and relax.

Move your eyes to focus as far upwards to the right and then downwards to the left.

Bring your eyes back to the centre and relax.

Look to the right as far you can go, followed by the left as far as you can go and then back to the centre and relax.

Finally, look up as far as you can go and then down as far as you can go.

Bring your eyes back to the centre and relax.

Be gentle with your eyes while performing these exercises and build up slowly.

Resistance bands / strong rubber bands are also very helpful in developing muscle strength.

They can be used in a variety of ways.

Attach the band to a solid object e.g. the doorknob of a locked door.

Holding the band firmly, pull yourself away from the door.

You can also attach the band to the arms of your wheelchair, or the arms of a chair or a solid stable object, (if you are not wheelchair bound).

Pull the band towards you with your palms facing upwards and then repeat this exercise with your palms facing downwards.

You can also pull the band crossways across your chest.

Pretend you are playing a piano.

Use all your fingers to increase dexterity.

You might find this easier to do if you listen to music and why not tap your feet at the same time?

You could also pretend you are conducting an orchestra.

In this way your exercise routine can be both beneficial and enjoyable.

In a seated position, bend over as far as you can as if you were picking something up off the ground, bending only as far as is comfortable for you.

Over time you will find you can reach a little bit further.

In a seated position, raise your right leg, with knee bent, as far upwards as you can.

You can use your hands to help you achieve this.

Return your foot to the ground then do likewise with your left leg.

Exercise is designed to build up your muscles.

Be careful not to overdo any exercise.

If you feel strained whilst doing any of the above, stop the exercise immediately.

Exercise is most beneficial when repeated on a regular basis giving regard to your fitness level at the outset, and allowing yourself time to recover between sessions.

Focusing on the physical activity of your choice releases the mind even temporarily, from the treadmill of anxiety and stress.

Mindfulness

Learn to relax and live in the present.

No matter how much we would like to, we cannot change what happened in the past, but we can learn from it. There is little point in stressing and worrying about what has happened, or what might happen in the future.

If you were on a sun holiday a month ago, you wore suitable light clothing.

If you are going on a skiing holiday next month, you will wear suitable attire for the cold conditions.

If today is a fairly cool rainy day, you are dressed for the weather TODAY, as neither your swimsuit nor your skiing gear is appropriate.

In other words you are dressed for the NOW.

NOW train yourself to think and live in the NOW

Mindfulness is the capacity to be aware of what is going on in your life NOW.

You can be mindful at any time and in any place.

It simply means bringing your awareness to the task in hand, whether that's washing the dishes, doing the shopping, going to work, or enjoying a good book.

Practise being mindful and it soon becomes automatic.

For example, sit quietly in your living room.

Breathe normally.

There is no need to change your breathing pattern.

Just be aware of your breathing.

Notice how your clothes touch your body.

Notice how your body touches the chair.

Be aware of the familiar sounds inside your house for a few moments e.g. (a kettle boiling, a clock ticking, pipes creaking, a radio or television in the background, people speaking in another room).

Then concentrate on the sounds outside your house, like the birds singing, or traffic moving or children playing.

Bring your awareness back to the familiar indoor sounds.

Notice how your body touches the chair and how your clothes touch your body.

Finally be aware of your own breathing.

For those few moments you have stopped your mind wandering and yet you have been totally mindful.

If you practise being mindful fairly regularly, then you will find it easier to incorporate it into your daily routines.

Believe it or not, you are actually being mindful at this very moment while reading this book.

Mindfulness is non-judgemental.

It is simply observing without criticism everything going on around you, including your feelings, thoughts and emotions via your senses.

Being mindful allows you to savour life's precious moments and to participate fully in the here and now.

For example, mindful eating is a very helpful tool for those with an eating disorder or those choosing a healthy lifestyle.

Mindful driving ensures safety.

It is easy to be mindful when you are engaged in a hobby or activity that captures your imagination and focuses your attention one hundred percent.

Take for example a golfer teeing off.

They know they must position their body in a certain way and use a certain technique to achieve the desired outcome.

They are totally present in the moment.

They cannot afford to break their concentration.

This is mindfulness.

On the other hand, it is much more difficult to develop and practise the skill of mindfulness when you are performing mundane tasks i.e. dressing, showering and brushing your teeth, doing housework or the myriad of other tasks, when your mind seems to wander off at tangents all on its own.

Performing daily routines becomes automatic and allows the mind to wander unchecked.

When this happens, you simply observe what is distracting you, label it as a thought, a feeling or emotion, then gently bring your mind and focus back to the task at hand in the here and now.

This is mindfulness.

Practising mindfulness brings many benefits to your physical, emotional and mental well-being.

You can be mindful at any time, reducing stress and anxiety with immediate effect and with practise this will result in improved relationships and self-confidence.

If you lead a busy life and you are unable to find a quiet place to relax and be mindful, you can always do the following simple deep-breathing mindfulness exercise.

This is most helpful and effective, especially if you are feeling stressed when on the go.

Focus on your breathing.

Breathe in slowly through your nose all the way down to your tummy and exhale through your mouth.

Be aware of your breathing.

Use this exercise especially when feeling upset, as it has an immediate calming effect and will help to ease your anxiety and stress, helping you to get through the day.

The more you practise being mindful, the easier it becomes.

You can create your own mindfulness exercises to suit your lifestyle.

With practise the results will be greater and longer lasting.

Eventually, you will automatically deploy mindfulness exercises as a tool to manage bouts of stress and anxiety in your daily life.

Time spent in mindfulness is time well spent on nurturing yourself, helping you feel confident, calm and relaxed.

Mindfulness can bring you relaxation and freedom from stress and allows your inner peace to be revealed.

Mindfulness will not assist you in avoiding stressful difficulties, but rather it will help you to view them from a different perspective, almost as an observer.

This will free you from overreacting, sidestepping, or failing to address the issues and help you to face your challenges calmly and effectively, eliminating many of the thoughts that trigger your stressful responses.

Mindfulness empowers you to deal with events in your daily life in a constructive manner.

Meditation

Mindfulness is often considered to be a type of meditation.

It can be considered the first step on the road to meditation.

You can be mindful in any place at any time while performing routine tasks.

However, meditation is a task requiring total concentration, quieting your mind and freeing it from all distractions.

There are many forms of meditation, but for the purposes of this book, meditation is treated as an inwardly oriented practise, which you can do either by yourself or guided by instructions on a CD, or by attending a meditation class of your choice.

If you are feeling stressed or overloaded with worries and fears, meditation will help you become more present and more interactive with the people around you.

It will help you reduce the restlessness and agitation in your life and restore natural clarity and joy.

By practising meditation you will experience greater stillness and peace of mind, be more focused and more present to yourself and the significant others in your life.

The aim of meditation is to move your mind / thoughts away from logical thinking and get in touch with your subconscious, helping you to get to know yourself at a deeper level.

If you would like to try meditation and you don't know where to begin, there are numerous classes, books, CDs, DVDs and Apps available to assist you.

Find yourself a quiet, warm, comfortable environment, where you won't be disturbed for approximately thirty minutes.

Turn off phones, television or anything else which might disturb you.

Wear comfortable clothing.

Play soothing, relaxing, appropriate, background music.

Move away from your regular thinking patterns; take a mental step back; clear your mind and get some perspective.

Meditation is relaxing and very beneficial. It increases the blood flow, slows the heart rate and enhances the immune system. It helps you to focus on issues in the here and now.

Through meditation, you acknowledge your thoughts, fears and anxieties as if one step removed, letting your worries and concerns pass over you, like clouds in the sky, allowing you to maintain perspective.

Meditation assists in balancing the fight / flight or freeze response to stressful situations.

However, if you find yourself having stressful thoughts or feelings of distress during meditation, then it is advisable for you to cease the activity.

It is a personal choice and is not for everyone.

Religion and Spirituality

If you are not a member of an organised religion, or if you have no spiritual awareness and you don't believe in a Higher Power, then this section is not for you.

Skip to the next section.

There is a huge spiritual dimension at work in the lives of many people.

It is a personal choice for those who find it helpful to call for assistance from a Higher Power when experiencing anxiety and stress.

Your religious or spiritual belief system influences your core values and your behaviour.

Religious beliefs, or being part of a religious congregation, can provide a source of comfort in times of anxiety and stress.

Belief in a Higher Power helps people feel that they are not alone in their trials and tribulations and that there is always a power outside themselves, on which they can call to give their lives meaning and purpose.

Those who find consolation in religion trust that there is a Higher Power guiding them towards the greater good.

If this describes you, then embrace the positives of your professed faith through prayer, meditation, rituals or other expressions encouraged by your faith for your greater health and well-being and the good of those around you.

Although religion and spirituality are connected, they are also quite separate.

Many people who are not associated with any organised religion can be spiritual.

Spirituality is individual by its nature and means different things to different people.

It is an experience, a search for meaning and inner connectedness with the universe and the development of personal values.

Many deeply spiritual people approach spirituality from a humanistic perspective.

They strive for compassion, practise forgiveness and tolerance, altruism, connection with all creatures of the universe, inner peace and to live in harmony with the forces of the universe for the greater good of humanity.

Spiritual people have an awareness that all things present in the universe in the here and now are interconnected, purposeful and co-dependent.

Deeply spiritual people do not focus on the material world but rather find their inspiration and orientation through their interaction with the universe.

Likewise, deeply religious people trust that their Higher Power, along with members and resources of their religious community, will provide necessary support for them during stressful times.

You are the best placed to decide what nurtures your well-being and gives you meaning, purpose, hope and comfort and happiness in your life.

Neither religious nor spiritual beliefs justify avoidance from taking responsibility, or condone or excuse a person for destructive actions, feelings, words, or behaviour.

Reliance on spirituality and religion can be counter-productive when used as a defence mechanism against feeling, owning, expressing or taking responsibility for your painful negative feelings.

It's your choice

Do not overmedicate on prescription drugs or abuse substances.

Recall your most important achievements.

Close your eyes, remember what you were thinking and doing at that particular time and how it made you feel.

Resolve that this is the pattern that you will follow in the future in order to regain those positive feelings.

Anxiety reduces your confidence and makes it more difficult to do things that you once had no difficulty with.

You can regain your confidence by building on your strengths.

Set your goals in achievable steps in order to achieve success and boost your confidence.

Concentrate on the present, not on the past.

Volunteer to help others and enjoy the experience of helping others.

Part 3

Basic human needs common to all

Anxiety, stress, anger, hurt and fear are activated when you feel your needs are not being satisfied.

The following is a list of some of the main needs which are universal.

You need to feel:

Accepted	Seen
Acknowledged	Significant
Appreciated	Touched
Cared for	Treated fairly
Encouraged	Treated honestly
Heard	Treated with dignity
Held	Trusted
Loved	Valued
Respected	Understood
Safe	Useful

Healthy lifestyle choices

A healthy lifestyle, a nutritious diet, enough sleep and enough exercise will help you in your quest to manage your anxiety and stress.

Here is a list of some activities that will help you to live a healthy lifestyle:

- Go for leisurely walks
- Take a long luxurious bath
- Read a book
- Watch a film
- Dance
- Go to the cinema
- Dine with friends
- Go for a swim
- Chat with friends
- Participate in a sport
- Visit friends or family
- Listen to music or play a musical instrument
- Play with your pet
- Have fun
- Laugh

- Join a support group
- Socialise

The list is endless and can be designed to suit your personal taste.

It is a good idea for you to make a list of things that you find relaxing.

Make sure to include activities that do not necessarily cost money.

Monitor how often you take time to relax and show yourself that you care about you.

Evaluate your belief system

Humans process events according to their own belief system. This process automatically incorporates:

A) Thoughts .... *how I think*

B) Feelings .... *how I feel*

C) Behaviour ..... *what I do*

D) Physiology .....*how my body physically reacts*

For example, you are invited to spend the festive season with a family member, who has breached what you believe to be the acceptable norms of society e.g. a co-habiting, unmarried couple.

Their lifestyle goes against your deeply held beliefs.

You have two choices:

   (i) Refuse the invitation based on your own beliefs.

   (ii) You accept their invitation and enjoy yourself while still retaining your own beliefs but not imposing them on others.

(i) By refusing the invitation, you are judging others by your standards and belief system. You feel that you must adhere to your own beliefs. Your behaviour, in refusing the invitation, lets the couple know how you think and feel. Your body might be tensed up, your heart palpitating with the stress of your family member putting you in that position by inviting you in the first instance.

(ii) By reframing the situation and looking at it from a non-judgemental perspective, you decide to accept the invitation. Your thinking centres round accepting the rights of others to live by their belief system. You feel comfortable accepting the invitation without compromising your own beliefs. You accept gracefully and look forward to the event. Your body feels calm and relaxed.

Another simple example of beliefs and consequences is:

You are passing by a coffee shop and you observe two of your neighbours enjoying a coffee seated close to the window.

You wave at them and as they look in your direction they are both laughing.

(i) You think they are laughing at you. You feel stupid for waving at them in the first instance. You decide to speed up your pace and continue your journey red-faced with heart palpitating.

(ii) You think they are delighted to see you. You feel happy and you decide to go in and join them with a light-hearted step.

The previous three examples illustrate clearly the benefits of adopting a positive approach to life.

It is much better for you to get into the habit of thinking:

I can,

I will,

I am able,

Rather than focusing on the negatives:

I cannot,

I will not,

I am not able.

You are depriving yourself of joyful dialogue with others and perpetuating your anxiety and stress by engaging in negativity as outlined in items (i) above.

Acceptance of things you cannot change will necessitate you changing your mindset, and as a consequence, you reduce your anxiety and stress and focus on what you **can** change.

By taking control in this manner, you will empower yourself and live in harmony with those around you.

Changing your thinking

It is not easy to change your thinking, but with practise, it is possible.

The question you must ask yourself is: *"Do I really want or need to change my thinking in such a way as to decrease my anxiety and stress?"*

If your present thinking pattern is not working for you, then the answer is clearly yes.

By engaging in negative behaviour, isolating yourself or adopting what you consider safety mechanisms to cope with stressful situations, you are not facing your problem of anxiety and stress. Examples of this are:

- Refusing invitations and avoiding socialising with others
- Staying in
- Avoiding supermarkets or public places at busy times
- Always shopping online
- Only going out in the company of a close companion
- Showing up for brief periods of time at events and making excuses for fast exits

- Always having a drink, mobile phone, cigarette in hand or fidgeting with hair, clothes or handbag
- Avoiding eye contact with others
- Self-medication

If you depend on the above strategies to cope with stressful situations, you will remain stuck, your belief system will stay intact and you will not alleviate your anxiety and stress.

It is essential for you to reframe situations, focus on the positive, allow for alternate views and change your behaviour.

This in turn will help to enhance your relationships, help you to feel healthier and happier and will reduce the anxiety and stress in your daily life.

If you are thinking happy thoughts, smiling, feeling light-hearted and relaxed physically, you are not experiencing anxiety or stress or panic.

It is not easy to change the four components of your total behaviour i.e. thinking, doing, feeling and physical.

However, by taking control of your thinking and

your doing, this in turn will affect your feelings and your physical reactions.

In other words, if you want to reduce your anxiety and stress, begin by changing what you are thinking and what you are doing and do what you are able to do in the circumstances.

Imagine you are on the way to a job interview.

You have prepared well for the interview, dressed appropriately and left your home in plenty of time and are waiting for public transport.

A passing truck destroys your clothes with mucky water. How could you take control in this situation?

You could phone your potential employer, explain your situation and ask for a later appointment to enable you to go home and change.

You can make simple changes to ease your stress and anxiety, some of which will make you smile.

If you are left-handed, try to open a tin of soup, draw a picture or write with your right hand.

What are the results?

Where are the contents of the can?

Are you the new Picasso?

Is your writing legible and in a straight line?

Highly unlikely, but can you see the funny side of your action?

Think about your decision to try something new.

You have succeeded in using a part of your brain that you don't normally use for these tasks and you have relaxed even for a few short moments.

You achieved this by allowing yourself the opportunity to try something new without any internal pressure.

Visualise yourself as a tennis player.

You are on the court at the start of the game.

You look across the net and instead of one opponent, you visualise yourself playing against two or more.

You're thinking to yourself, "what is going to happen next? Which of these opponents is going to strike the ball first and which direction is it going to go?"

All of these thoughts are racing through your

mind before anyone strikes a ball.

One serves, then the next person serves.

You can't decide which ball to respond to so you end up falling down in a heap because you are understandably unable to cope with balls coming at you at the same time from different directions.

The only way to play a match like this is to insist on following the rules and playing against one opponent at a time.

This allows you to use your skills and expertise in tackling one challenger at a time.

You can apply the same analogy to your life.

Don't try to take on everything at once.

Set yourself targets and challenge one problem at a time before you move on to the next one.

Solving the small problems first will empower you and motivate you going forward.

Ask for assistance if you need it. People will be glad to help you.

If you have alienated others when stressed in the past, apologise, explain your situation and move forward.

You are not superhuman.

Take breaks when you need them and return to the task at hand refreshed and energised.

The longest journey begins with the first step.

If you are driving a car on a dark country road, you can only see a couple of hundred yards in front of you lit up by the headlights.

You cannot see ahead to the journey's end but you drive along happily and contentedly knowing you will get there in the end.

Do not stress yourself thinking too far ahead.

Deal with what you can do right now.

Confine your thinking to the present moment and the task at hand and you will ease your stress and achieve so much more.

Overcome the power of negative thinking

Do you catastrophize? Do you blow things out of proportion without asking yourself; *"where is the evidence?"*

Do you always expect the worst outcome?

Do you make judgements without supporting information, for example thinking to yourself, *"nobody likes me?"*

Could your thinking possibly be distorted?

For example, if your partner dumps you, do you take it personally, thinking there is something wrong with you and that you will never have another relationship and nobody else will be interested in you?

To a lesser extent, if some stranger is rude to you in the course of the day, for example a shop assistant, a bank teller, or a taxi driver, do you take it personally, thinking that you must have done something wrong, when in fact they may be having a bad day?

Do you find yourself apologising all the time?

Are you selective in your thinking and tend to focus on a single negative incident for example, one individual's sneering look, as opposed to all the happy smiling faces you encountered at a particular function?

Do you over-generalise believing that if you make a mistake once, you will repeat the same error for evermore?

Is your thinking black and white with no grey areas?

Do you think that everyone is either all good or all bad including yourself?

Do you label yourself and others?

Examples of this are thinking that all blondes are dumb and all redheads are fiery. Worse still, do you label yourself as being an awkward person merely because you feel awkward in a particular situation?

Do you take people's negative criticism of you on board? For example, if someone calls you stupid, do you believe them and accept that label for yourself without question?

Do you assume responsibility for other people's happiness?

Are you the type of person who notices someone at the other end of the dinner table who needs the salt before they even ask for it themselves?

Do you take the blame when something happens to others, thus relieving others of taking responsibility for their own actions?

Do you rescue people as opposed to supporting them, thus adding to your own anxiety and stress?

Become aware of how often you judge yourself harshly. How often do you use the words?

I should have,

I must,

I ought to,

I have to,

I could have,

I never,

Nobody cares about me,

I am worthless.

If so then you need to challenge, reassess and change your negative thinking.

How do you train yourself to look at things from a different perspective and rethink your negative thoughts?

Ask yourself how would I think about this if I was having a good day? How would I advise someone else in this situation? Is there any other way of looking at this particular situation? Ask a trusted friend or your doctor or counsellor if they think your thinking is distorted.

What are the facts of the case? What is the evidence? Are you looking at the big picture? Look for evidence that highlights the reality of the situation and makes you feel better.

Can you find several explanations in order to come up with the right answers for you?

Step back and make a conscious decision not to allow yourself to be drawn into negative thinking about yourself or others by negative people close to you.

Ask yourself: *"What is the worst thing that could happen? Is it likely to happen? What can I do if it happens? How can I get help?"*

Look at a person you admire. Take note of their coping skills and model yourself on them.

Use your imaginary crystal ball with positive effect by looking into the future thinking: *"I have coped in the past, I can cope now and I will cope in the future."*

Develop the habit of keeping a thought record, tracking your progress and building your skills and changing your attitude.

Even if you lapse from time to time, your progress record will act as a motivator in your quest to reduce anxiety and stress in your life and empower you to lead a more fulfilling productive life.

Notice how thinking positively has yielded better results for you and reduced your anxiety and stress.

Notice the consequences of your thoughts and actions and continue to do what is working for you.

Evaluate yourself continuously asking yourself: *"What could I do differently?*

What action could I take to be more effective?"

Practise makes perfect.

Effective Communication

We communicate with each other through our words, our tone of voice, our body language and facial expressions.

Bottling up your emotions adds to your stress. The old adage 'A problem shared is a problem halved' is true.

If you are concerned about your health, relationships or financial worries, talk to someone you can really trust, whether it is a friend or a professional.

How we feel about ourselves has a direct bearing on how we relate to others. Conversation is a two way process, so be prepared to talk and listen.

When you are listening, try to focus on what the other person is saying, rather than thinking about what you are going to say next.

Listen carefully in order to avoid misinterpretation, ambiguity or potential disagreements. This is particularly relevant when communicating with people from different cultures.

Do not underestimate the value of confiding in someone you trust, when you are in need of support.

Try not to be too self-conscious. We all experience stress from time to time. Make eye contact and speak slowly, explaining your situation as clearly as you can.

Think about what you want to say; be honest and respectful to yourself and others.

When listening to others, allow yourself time to consider what you are hearing.

You may need to ask questions to understand fully what is being said.

Be open-minded and non-judgemental.

If you feel that you have not expressed yourself clearly, say so and start again.

Use humour and silence when appropriate.

If you are sharing something very personal to you, then it is important for you to stress the need for confidentiality, (provided you are not disclosing information pertinent to illegal activity).

You must also respect the rights of others to confidentiality.

Being able to express your feelings, disappointments and joys is essential to good mental health.

Effective communication is a key component of good interpersonal relationships.

Challenge Yourself

If you were happy with your life at present, you would not be reading this book. Reading this book alone will not change any part of your life, unless you choose to adopt some of its strategies, or others that you could, or might find useful in your situation.

This book is similar to a cookery book. Unless you decide to cook some of the recipes you will not taste the delicious food available to you.

As we said in our introduction, you are the best placed to decide what is best for you in your life.

If you continue to do things in the same way as you have always done, how can you possibly expect different results?

Once again, you can apply the cooking analogy.

If you use the same ingredients, prepare and cook your food in the same way at the same temperature, you can expect the same results.

Do you want your life to change?

What are you prepared to contribute to the change?

It is important to remember that the only person that you can change is yourself. You cannot change others, but you will find that when **you** change, those around you will change towards you.

There are some things in life that you cannot change, such as loss. This could be the loss of a person, pet, relationship, job, home, or financial security, but you can always change your responses to what life throws at you and learn acceptance.

By changing your thinking around the impact of loss, you can move forward and re-engage in enjoying your life.

Real change takes time, patience and practise.

Evaluate where you are at right now.

What would you like your life to be like? What areas do you need to focus on to achieve your goals?

It is advisable for you to focus on one objective at a time, beginning with the most pressing.

Look at the strategies in this book and decide to design your own personal step by step roadmap / approach to achieve your desired outcome.

Once you have worked out a plan, stick with it.

Make sure to take small, achievable steps.

As you progress in fulfilling your aims and objectives, little by little, you will gain in confidence.

Your mental health and well-being is defined by how you feel about yourself, how you feel about others and how you are able to meet the demands of everyday life.

To maximise your progress, it is important to have balance in your life.

Taking care of your nutritional needs and being careful not to abuse substances such as caffeine, alcohol, nicotine and / or drugs.

This enhances your energy levels and gives you the motivation to live your life to the full.

Make sure to fulfil your need for leisure time and fun too.

Incorporate a gentle regime of exercise in order to relieve stress and tension and stimulate the release of endorphins, a chemical which gives us a natural feeling of health and well-being.

If self-doubt is causing you problems, challenge yourself to replace negative self-talk and self-doubt with encouraging and positive messages e.g. I can, I will, I am able.

Each morning on rising, determine to make the most of what you have throughout the day.

Start this process by paying attention to your personal grooming and dress and endeavour to maintain an upright positive posture.

This strategy in itself starts you off with confidence and demonstrates your confidence to those with whom you engage during the course of the day.

Greet yourself in the mirror with a smile.

Life is challenging.

Realising and accepting that there are things in life over which we have no control, frees us to focus on areas we can change.

If you feel under pressure and that implementing these strategies is overwhelming, then it is advisable to seek professional help.

Continuous Evaluation

We strongly recommend that you examine your thoughts / actions regularly with the help of the questions posed in this book in a non-judgemental way.

As your awareness shifts, other insights which you may have overlooked or denied may surface in your consciousness.

With the confidence gained through the use of this book, you will now feel empowered to tackle new challenges as they arise.

There are many components of good mental health and well-being.

These include: self-esteem, diet, sleep, effective communication, relaxation, exercise and good interpersonal relationships.

Monitor your progress in terms of your short-term goals. Have you achieved them?

Do you need to update your plan to continually challenge yourself in order to progress to your ultimate goals?

Have you built at least twenty minutes relaxation into your daily routine?

Have you made an entry in your journal lately?

By checking your journal you may be surprised at how far you have progressed.

Your journal entries will give you an insight into the areas you need to focus on.

Don't be too hard on yourself if you haven't followed your plan consistently.

Perhaps your original plan was overly ambitious. Be decisive about what you want to change.

Prioritise and don't try to do everything at once.

Go back to the basics and draw up a new plan of small achievable steps.

Remember you are only human and resolve to re-engage with your new plan for a more balanced lifestyle. In order to maintain general physical health, we recommend a healthy lifestyle and regular medical check-ups.

You may also benefit from other books in the ***Empower Yourself Series.***

Summary

Life is not perfect for anyone, but it is possible to train yourself to meet its challenges as they arise.

Life is meant to be enjoyed rather than endured.

Nothing stays the same and you can learn to adapt to new situations.

You can empower yourself to achieve your full potential in an ever changing world.

Value yourself and don't forget to pat yourself on the back and take credit for every little success and achievement along your road to managing your anxiety and stress.

This will have a positive effect and encourage you to move to the next stage.

By following the steps in this guide, you can learn to live a full life without engaging in destructive responses to anxiety and stress.

However if your reflections and self-evaluations reveal deeper concerns that continue to cause you problems, then it's advisable for you to seek therapy from a professional.

Regular medical check-ups are essential to rule out any physical conditions that may be causing your anxiety and stress.

This reassurance will help reduce your stress levels and motivate you to adopt the strategies in the *Empower Yourself Series*.

We wish you every success in managing your anxiety / stress.
Life is for living! So make the most of it!

Your future is in your hands.

Empower Yourself

Illustrator

Teresa Howes

I was born in Ballyfermot, Dublin and educated in Inchicore. I am presently a third year honours student in Art and Design Education at the National College of Art and Design, Dublin, Ireland. I am a former student of Dr. Robert. When she approached me with regard to illustrations for the *Empower Yourself Book Series* I was so excited to be given such a fantastic opportunity.

The authors had a concept for character representations for their books and in collaboration with them I created and designed the illustrations. Although the illustrations are cartoon characters, their purpose is to show the emotion behind the presenting issue, whilst at the same time not demeaning the seriousness of the topics involved.

This is my first professional commission. I am delighted to be involved with Burke Robert Publishing Ltd. and I look forward to a successful future with the authors.

Teresa

E-mail address: t.howes2308@gmail.com

Books in the
Empower Yourself Series

~~~~~~~~~~~~~~~

Say Goodbye to Panic Attacks

Manage your Anger

Manage your Anxiety and Stress

~~~~~~~~~~~~~~~

Visit our online store at

www.burkerobertpublishing.com